DO YOU REALLY WANT TO MEET EDMONTOSAURUS?

BY ANNETTE BAY PIMENTEL • ILLUSTRATED BY DANIELE FABBRI

AMICUS ILLUSTRATED and AMICUS INK
are published by Amicus
P.O. Box 1329, Mankato, MN 56002
www.amicuspublishing.us

EDITOR: Alissa Thielges
SERIES DESIGNER: Kathleen Petelinsek
BOOK DESIGNER: Veronica Scott

LIBRARY OF CONGRESS CATALOGING-IN-PUBLICATION DATA
Names: Pimentel, Annette Bay, author. | Fabbri, Daniele, 1978-
    illustrator.
Title: Do you really want to meet Edmontosaurus? / by Annette
    Bay Pimentel ; illustrated by Daniele Fabbri.
Description: Mankato, Minnesota : Amicus Illustrated and
    Amicus Ink, [2020] | Series: Do you really want to meet a
    dinosaur? | Audience: K to grade 3. | Includes bibliographical
    references.
Identifiers: LCCN 2018039668 (print) | LCCN 2018040766 (ebook)
    | ISBN 9781681517926 (pdf) | ISBN 9781681517100 (library
    binding) | ISBN 9781681524962 (pbk.)
Subjects: LCSH: Edmontosaurus--Juvenile literature. |
    Dinosaurs--Juvenile literature.
Classification: LCC QE862.065 (ebook) | LCC QE862.065 P558
    2020 (print) | DDC 567.914--dc23
LC record available at https://lccn.loc.gov/2018039668

Printed in the United States of America
HC 10 9 8 7 6 5 4 3 2 1
PB 10 9 8 7 6 5 4 3 2 1

ABOUT THE AUTHOR
Annette Bay Pimentel lives in Moscow, Idaho with her family.
She doesn't have a time machine, so she researches the
past at the library. She writes about what happened a
long time ago in nonfiction picture books like Mountain Chef
(2016, Charlesbridge). You can visit her online at
www.annettebaypimentel.com.

ABOUT THE ILLUSTRATOR
Daniele Fabbri was born in Ravenna, Italy, in 1978. He
graduated from Istituto Europeo di Design in Milan,
Italy, and started his career as a cartoon animator,
storyboarder, and background designer for animated
series. He has worked as a freelance illustrator since 2003,
collaborating with advertising agencies and international
publishers, including many books for Amicus.

Look at that long, strong tail. Imagine the dinosaur swinging it. What a wallop! You want to see it in action? It could do some damage. Do you really want to meet an Edmontosaurus?

They're extinct. You'll need a
time machine to meet one. Go
back 70 million years to the
Cretaceous Period. Head north.
Canada was warmer back then.
But you'll still need a jacket
and hat. Take a flashlight, too.

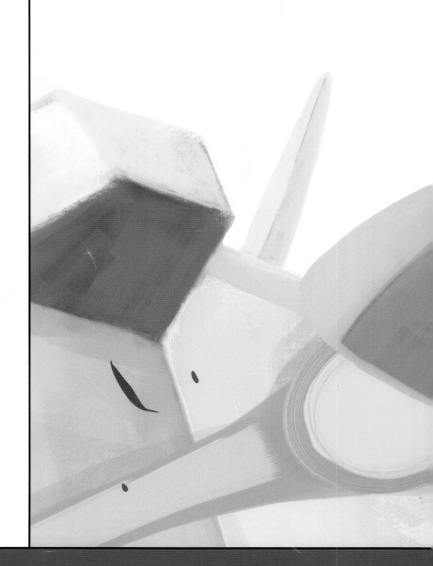

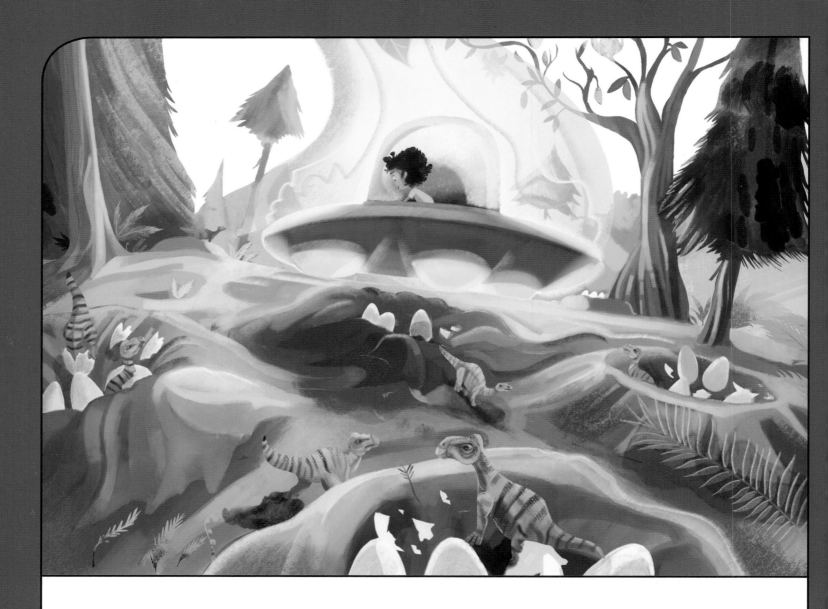

Look! Those are Edmontosaurus nests. Most of the eggs have already hatched. But some baby dinosaurs are still in their nests.

What cuties! An Edmontosaurus hatchling is 20 inches (51 cm) long and 8 inches (20 cm) tall. That's about the height of a toaster.

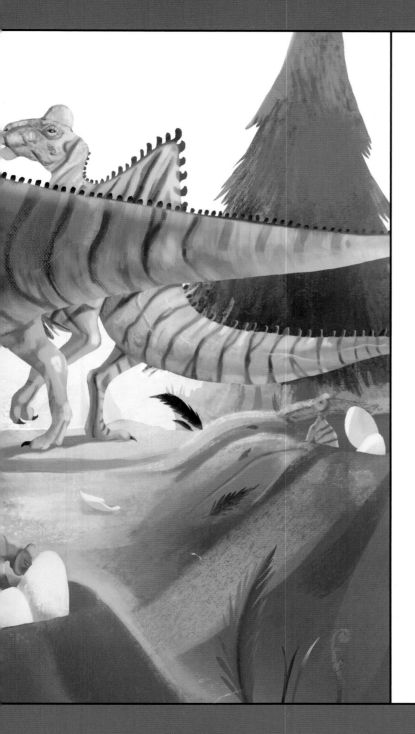

Adults come back to the nests. They have food for the babies. At 30 feet (9 m) long, they are big but gentle. The adults may bump into each other. But don't worry, they won't step on the babies.

Brrrr. It's chilly. Pull on your hat. Edmontosaurus doesn't mind the cold. But the plants it eats need sunshine to grow.

This far north, winter days are dark. So the dinosaur herd migrates, heading south. You can keep up. They only walk about 1 mile (1.6 km) per hour.

Edmontosaurus has a fleshy dome on its head. The dome helps dinosaurs recognize each other. It also helps make this dinosaur good-looking to another Edmontosaurus!

Edmontosaurus grazes as it walks. It pulls off bark and cones with its hooked beak. It especially loves horsetail plants. Its jaw waggles from side to side, grinding the food between its teeth.

The sun is setting. Move closer. See the small dinosaurs? They hatched earlier this summer. And they are already bigger than you! Edmontosauruses grow fast.

You hear a noise in the forest. Switch on your flashlight. Uh-oh. You are not the only one watching the dinosaurs. An Albertosaurus, a fierce carnivore, is eyeing them, too. This Edmontosaurus herd is in danger!

The adults see the meat-eater. To protect the young, the herd works together. They circle the small dinosaurs.

Dinosaurs at the edge of the group swing their tails. They kick and bash. This meat-eater gives up and runs away.

Your flashlight flickers. The batteries are dying. You can't see anything more tonight, but that's okay. You met an Edmontosaurus and saw a herd of them. Time to head home. Stay safe, Edmontosaurus herd!

WHERE HAVE EDMONTOSAURUS FOSSILS BEEN FOUND?

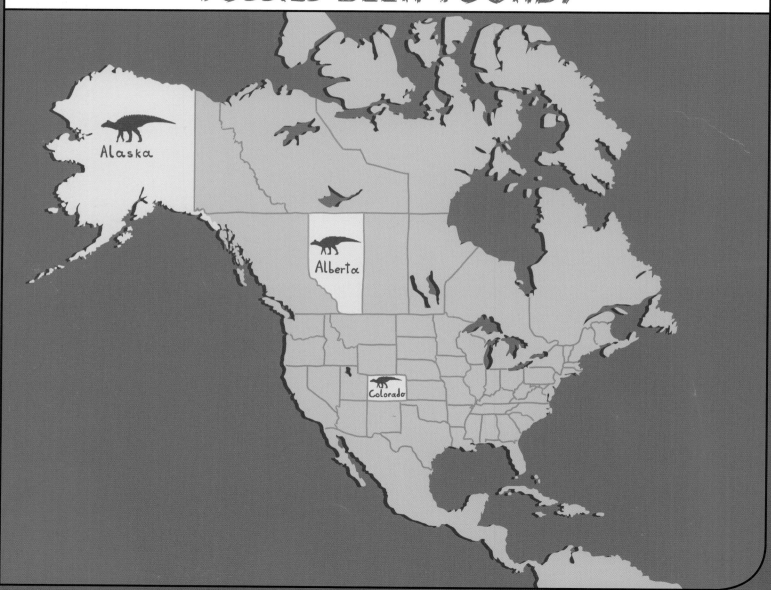

Alaska

Alberta

Colorado

GLOSSARY

carnivore—An animal that eats other animals.

Cretaceous Period—The time between 145.5 and 65.5 million years ago.

hatchling—A young animal soon after it comes out of an egg.

herd—A group of animals that feed and travel together.

migrate—To move from one place to another according to the season.

AUTHOR'S NOTE

Time machines aren't real, of course. But the details of Edmontosaurus in this book are based on research. Scientists study fossils and make educated guesses as to how dinosaurs looked and acted. For example, in 2013, a paleontologist found a skull that was pressed in mud. From this fossil, scientists realized that Edmontosaurus had a dome on its head. New dinosaur discoveries are made every year. Look up the books and websites below to learn more.

READ MORE

DK Publishing. *Dinosaurs: A Visual Encyclopedia.* New York: Penguin Random House, 2018.

Peterson, Megan Cooley. *Dinosaurs.* Mankato, Minn.: Black Rabbit Books, 2017.

Rissman, Rebecca. *Edmontosaurus and Other Duck-Billed Dinosaurs.* North Mankato, Minn.: Capstone, 2017.

WEBSITES

DENALI'S CRETACEOUS MURAL
https://www.nps.gov/dena/learn/nature/cretaceous-mural.htm
Click on the mural to learn more about Alaska during the Cretaceous time.

DK FIND OUT! EDMONTOSAURUS
https://www.dkfindout.com/us/dinosaurs-and-prehistoric-life/dinosaurs/edmontosaurus/
Facts about what this dinosaur looked like.

Every effort has been made to ensure that these websites are appropriate for children. However, because of the nature of the Internet, it is impossible to guarantee that these sites will remain active indefinitely or that their contents will not be altered.